FREDERIK IV

King on
his Own Terms

by Jens Gunni Busck

Historika

Published in cooperation with the Royal Danish Collection

CONTENTS

The coat of arms of the realm as it appeared in the time of Frederik IV. It is a part of the stucco ceiling of the Great Hall at Rosenborg Palace and was made in the early eighteenth century, when the King often used that little pleasure palace. Frederik IV gradually began spending more time at his own pleasure palaces, Frederiksberg and Fredensborg and he is the last king to use Rosenborg as a residence.

THE PERSONAL ABSOLUTE MONARCHY

Frederik IV was the first king of Denmark-Norway who was born with the right to inherit the throne and absolute power. He certainly rose to the challenge. None of Denmark's other absolute monarchs ruled in such a headstrong manner as Frederik IV. He came close to realising the ideal of personal absolute power: that the King decides everything not only in theory but in practice. He also set new standards with regard to what a king could get away with in his love life. The King entered into two morganatic marriages, and the second time he even abducted his beloved from her home and then made her Queen.

Denmark-Norway's first two absolute monarchs, Frederik III and Christian V, had created a state in which power had been centralized to an extent that had never been seen before and in which the King himself for the most part could determine the political options that would be available to him. Frederik IV chose an approach that was basically simple: he took away the decision-making power of officials in the state's central administration and made all decisions related to matters of state himself whenever this was possible. This meant taking on a huge amount of work, but the King had an enormous capacity for such work despite the fact that he was a small and slender man. He worked tirelessly at his desk when he was not travelling around the country to make sure that things were functioning and that his orders were being followed. This concentration of power could have been problematic in the hands of many other individuals, but Frederik IV administered it conscientiously and was popular with the populace.

The King's popularity was by no means decreased by the fact that the King got Denmark-Norway through the Great Northern War without bringing a great

Equestrian statue of Frederik IV in the costume of a Roman imperator with a laurel wreath, which reflects the standard model for the royal equestrian statues of the age. Frederik IV received the statue as a New Year present from Queen Louise in 1701; it was made in Copenhagen by the goldsmith Andreas Norman.

deal of destruction upon the realm. The war was otherwise a long and bloody affair, and Frederik IV was just as unsuccessful in his attempts to reconquer Scania, Blekinge, and Halland as Christian V had been during the Scanian War. On the other hand, he did succeed in incorporating the Schleswig parts of Gottorp into the Danish-Norwegian realm, a goal that had long been pursued by the kings of Denmark-Norway, and in finally securing a peace agreement with Sweden that had the potential to last.

Frederik IV's commitments in connection with governing the realm and the prosecution of the war meant that the King rarely took time for recreational activities, but this was not because he did not enjoy such activities. He was a dedicated dancer who loved opera and masquerade balls, and he twice visited his beloved Italy. His travels gave him inspiration for both masquerades and baroque gardens at home in Denmark, and with the construction of buildings such as Frederiksberg Palace and Fredensborg Palace, Frederik IV gave Danish architecture a new touch of southern elegance.

Frederik IV's marriages, however, were a particularly unusual feature of his reign. It was not in itself precedent-setting that he neglected his own queen, Louise, and had relationships with other women, but it was without precedent that the King concluded so-called morganatic marriages with two of them— while he was married to the Queen. It was even more controversial that after the death of Queen Louise he made his other wife, Anna Sophie Reventlow, Queen. She was only a noblewoman, that is, she was not a member of a princely family by birth, and the King's decision to enhance her status led to serious conflicts within the royal family. In his love life, as in other areas of his life, Frederik IV made his own rules.

An unspoiled upbringing

Prince Frederik was born at Copenhagen Castle on 11 October 1671 as the first-born child from the marriage of Christian V and Queen Charlotte Amalie. Just over ten years earlier, the prince's paternal grandfather, Frederik III, had introduced hereditary and absolute monarchy, and upon his death in 1670, Christian V had become King as the first person to accede to the throne by right of inheritance and therefore without a preceding election. In contrast to his new-

born son, however, Christian V had not been the heir to the throne from birth, and this was something that was considered important. Cannons were fired, church bells were rung all over the country, and prisoners were even released on this happy occasion.

For the mother, the birth was a relief for a special reason. The twenty-one-year-old Queen Charlotte Amalie had waited a year before she had become pregnant, and as the child to whom she had now given birth was a boy, she had fulfilled her dynastic duty as Queen. The Crown Prince did not see much of her, however, for she was a Calvinist, and because the successor to the throne was to be brought up in the Lutheran faith, he was kept at a distance from the Queen during his early childhood. The boy lived mostly at Copenhagen Castle and was raised by a noblewoman and widow named Cecilie Grubbe (the sister of Marie Grubbe, who would later become famous). From an early age, he also spent time in the second home his father had right next to Copenhagen Castle. The same year the Crown Prince was born, Christian V installed his mistress here, and he thus led a double family life with children who were about the same age in two homes. The children of the King's mistress became the Crown Prince's playmates, and it might well be that the father's views regarding his duties as a husband provided an example that influenced the son.

Strangely enough, the King found it appropriate that his son learn as little as possible, believing that learning interferes with common sense. Christian V himself was in no way oriented towards book-learning, and he did not wish his son to develop tendencies that went in that direction. As King, after all, he would have a body of administrators including well-informed advisors on whom he could rely, so there was no reason to fill the boy's head with knowledge that could confuse his judgment, Christian V felt. Thanks to this dubious logic, the Crown Prince received a very poor education. He learned a little about history, economics, art, and science, but this was limited to what was absolutely necessary, and his composition exercises by no means taught him to master the written languages he would require for his government work. The prince's first language was Danish, and his schooling was conducted in Ger-

Christening set in gold, made in Hamburg in about 1650. The set was first used at the baptism of Frederik IV in 1671 and has been used ever since when new Danish princes and princesses have been born. With the advent of absolute monarchy, a royal birth became a state matter; the Queen gave birth in public, and the child was baptised the same day. The christening set was probably intended to be a splendid toiletry set but was repurposed because it was of gold.

man (the language most commonly spoken at the court), but he never learned to write either of these languages at a level that would have been appropriate for a king. On the other hand, he later learned both French and Italian, and as an adult, he took many other steps to make up for not having received an adequate education as a child.

While the prince was growing up, the Scanian War (1675–79) was fought; after a great deal of bloodshed, this war ended with a return to the status quo. He could hardly have avoided hearing about his father's continual efforts to eliminate the threat from the duchy of Gottorp, which consisted of several scattered areas within the duchies of Schleswig and Holstein and was an ally of Sweden. In reality, this was a hostile state within the King's territory, and one of his son's important tasks would be to find a solution to this problem—an undertaking in which he would in fact succeed.

It is also conceivable that the Crown Prince grew up hearing about the all-dominating chancellor of the realm Peter Griffenfeld, whom Christian V chose to topple from power in 1676, and who spent the rest of his life in prison. In becoming an admirer of the fallen chancellor of the realm, the Crown Prince may have been rebelling against his father, and Griffenfeld's example may have inspired Frederik IV to become an even more headstrong ruler than Griffenfeld himself.

It must have made a strong impression on the Crown Prince that when he reached his twenties most of his siblings and half-siblings had died already. He must have found remaining alive to be a real privilege—not least because the oldest known description of him (from a Swedish envoy's report to his king) describes the thirteen-year-old Crown Prince as pale and weak. The description also mentions, however, that he was alert, well-behaved, and self-assured in his speech and comportment.

The encounter with Italy

Just as his father had been, Prince Frederik was sent on a journey abroad that was intended to make him a man of the world. However, the focus of this journey was not the courts of Europe's absolute monarchs but Italy. The prince be-

Crown Prince Frederik during a so-called carousel ride—a discipline in which his father probably would have liked to see him engage with greater enthusiasm. The goal was to strike various things with lances, sword, and pistols, and here the prince has struck the head of a "Moor." It should be noted that this was not a real head.

gan his journey down through Europe in January 1692 with a relatively modest entourage of twenty-eight persons; the prince was travelling incognito, and overnight stays in royal seats were carefully avoided. The passage through the Alps, which was not without its dangers, was managed without any problems, and a month after leaving Denmark, the company reached Venice. For the Danish prince, the encounter with Italy was a watershed event.

His incognito status turned out to be impossible to maintain while participating in Venetian social life, so attempts to remain incognito were in reality abandoned—just as his father had abandoned his own attempts to remain anonymous when he had visited London and Paris as a young man. The prince was better able to remain incognito during his subsequent visit to Rome, where the Pope very discreetly provided a great deal of help to the prince and his retinue, and after six eventful weeks during which the prince encountered art and culture and made new acquaintances, the company proceeded to Siena, Livorno, Pisa, Florence, Lucca, and Genova. At that time, the court of the Medici in Florence was the only court of importance in Italy, and here nothing was done to obscure the identity of the successor to the Danish-Norwegian throne, who participated in all the splendid social events the city could offer.

The little crucifix that Maddalena Trenta gave Crown Prince Frederik, which he is supposed to have worn until his death. We cannot know whether the brief meeting in Lucca was of great significance to the young people, but it is certainly a good story.

Crown Prince Frederik, painted by Hyacinthe Rigaud during the Crown Prince's stay in Paris in 1693.

Of course, the twenty-year-old prince was attracted to the opposite sex, and there are several stories concerning his erotic adventures during his Italian journey, but it is difficult to say what is true in this regard. While in Florence, he is supposed to have had a relationship with a certain Countess Velo, and during the Crown Prince's three-day stay in Lucca the prince and a beautiful twenty-two-year-old noblewoman named Maddalena Trenta are supposed to have fallen madly in love with each other. He is said to have given her a portrait of himself and to have received in return a little silver crucifix that is kept at Rosenborg and that, according to the story, he always wore. The meeting with the Danish Crown Prince is even said to have caused Maddalena Trenta to enter a nunnery, for during his second journey to Italy in 1709, Frederik IV sought her out again and discovered that she had become a nun.

From Italy, the Crown Prince and his retinue travelled to France, where the prince spent July and August in Montpellier and the following two months in Angers. These were educational stays, for the prince spent his time learning French and practicing his riding to prepare for his subsequent stay at the court of the Sun King in Versailles. Crown Prince Frederik generally maintained his incognito status in France, for Louis XIV was at war with England, and in reality, Christian V was supporting both sides, so there was a desire to avoid having the prince's visit take on an overly official character. Outwardly, therefore, Louis XIV treated the prince as the Count of Schauenburg he was claiming to be, and the actual audience was brief, but the French king nevertheless arranged a splendid masquerade ball in Crown Prince Frederik's honour. As in Venice, the prince generally experienced an abundance of balls and masquerades in Paris and the surrounding area, and he would probably have liked to have stayed longer, but Christian V called him home, most likely because because the trip had become too expensive.

After farewell audiences with Louis XIV and the deposed English king James II, the company travelled north, and the Crown Prince had an opportunity to study the French fortifications. After this, the company's route took them through the Netherlands, where the prince was received splendidly in towns including Ghent and Brussels, and on the way through the Danish provinces, too, the prince's visits were appropriately celebrated. The company reached Copenhagen in April 1693.

A forced choice

Two years later, Christian V sent his son to Northern Germany so he could find an appropriate Protestant princess. Several candidates had previously been discussed, and one of those to whom Crown Prince Frederik had said no was one of the Swedish princesses who later, to the Danish King's regret, married

Prince Friedrich, the heir to Gottorp. If a Danish-Swedish marriage had become a reality, the history of the Nordic region would probably have looked very different, and this is only one of many examples that illustrate how decisive the dynastic marriages were.

The Crown Prince had been offered the option of choosing among the marriageable princesses of as many as six royal families, but he would end up visiting only the little court of Güstrow. This was due to a number of circumstances,

Queen Louise made these vases in wood with laque brillante (a lacquer technique that was very typical of this particular age) as a present for her husband.

the most important of which was that his younger brother Christian had died of smallpox shortly after having set forth on his grand tour. Because of this, Christian V called the Crown Prince home and commanded him to choose one of the four sisters in Güstrow, none of whom he found to be particularly attractive, and the prince chose Princess Louise, who was four years older than he. The Crown Prince is supposed to have explained this choice by saying that she seemed less troublesome than the others.

The couple had a splendid wedding in Copenhagen in December 1695 that lasted three days and cost Christian V about four barrels of gold. The bridegroom is not likely to have been enthusiastic, and while the bride was probably basically satisfied with the prospect of becoming the queen of Denmark-Norway, her life in Denmark ended up being anything but easy. Over the years, she gave birth to a total of five children, but she suffered because of her husband's publicly known relationships with other women. From home, she had brought a deep religiosity, and she would transfer this religiosity to her children—not least to her son Christian (VI). Her pious attitude does not seem to have had a calming influence on Queen Louise, however; she was known for her inappropriate attacks of rage against the King. She appears not to have had the ability to handle the King's infidelity well as Charlotte Amalie had when Christian V had established his double family life. Charlotte Amalie had been intellectually superior to her husband and had been able to occupy herself with running her estates and with many other things, but her successor had only her religion to compensate for the experience of being set aside by her husband. Louise was about as sad and isolated as a queen could be during the golden age of absolute monarchy.

On Valby Bakke

Already when he was nine years old, Crown Prince Frederik took over a four-winged farmhouse near what would later become Frederiksberg Runddel, two of the wings of which are still standing. Kaningården ("The Rabbit Farm"), as it was called, became a place where he liked to spend time, and it was also here he entertained friends and family. At that time, the estate lay fairly far out in the country, and after his journey abroad, the Crown Prince began serious work on making something out of the garden there, which had several fountains installed in it and was eventually enlarged to include the entire area that would eventually become the park Frederiksberg Have.

The hilltop south of the farm was an obviously appropriate site at which to construct a building in accordance with the southern style to which the Crown Prince had felt attracted on his journey. He developed his plan in consultation with Christian V, who had his own ambitious plans for the construction of a palace on the site where his mother's pleasure palace Sophie Amalienborg had burned—and where today's Amalienborg stands. Probably the Crown Prince himself influenced the drawings greatly, and construction began in 1699 with

Next spread: View of Frederiksberg Palace seen from the park Frederiksberg Have by J. J. Bruun, 1744. The palace was inaugurated in 1704 but expanded and heightened a few years later. This picture gives a sense of the park as designed by Frederik IV but shows the central elephant added by Christian VI, who also expanded the palace by adding two wings. Originally, all of Frederiksberg Have was characterised by the symmetrical Baroque style, elements of which are preserved today, but most of the park was relandscaped to become a Romantic garden around 1800.

economic support from Christian V. While construction was in progress, the house and the area were given the name Frederiksberg.

Christian V's own palace project did not become a reality during the King's own time, and one of the important reasons for this was the increasing danger of war. The King's nephew Friedrich, who had now become Duke of Gottorp, was making the King's life difficult by upgrading Gottorp's military forces and thus threatening Denmark-Norway. While the King was attempting to conclude alliances with Poland and Russia, he was also trying to arrange the marriage of his daughter Sophie Hedevig to the Swedish king, Charles XII, who had acceded to the Swedish throne as a fourteen-year-old in 1697. The King was not successful, and after the conclusion of the abovementioned marriage between the Swedish king's sister and the Duke of Gottorp, the prospects for the future for Christian V were not promising, not least because his health, which had never been particularly good, became extremely poor following a hunting accident in 1698.

A week before he died, Christian V must have realised that he would not make a complete recovery from his hunting injury, for he then finally invited his crown prince to attend the meetings of the Privy Council (a predecessor of the Council of State) and the Supreme Court. It had obviously been unwise of Frederik III not to have involved his eldest son in matters of state to a greater extent, and now Christian V had committed the same error. It is a well-known pattern in hereditary monarchies that incumbent kings have felt threatened by their sons, and probably this was the phenomenon at work in this case as well. Thanks to Christian V's attitude, Frederik IV was handicapped not only by a deficient education but also by a nearly complete lack of political experience when he acceded to the throne. This did not prevent him from doing a better job as King than anyone might reasonably have expected.

The accession and the first war

Frederik IV became King of Denmark-Norway the moment Christian V expired on 25 August 1699. His first major task as King was to give his father a magnificent funeral that demonstrated the God-given authority of the absolute monarchy. He was also presented with his father's political testament, which recommended that he should protect the absolute monarchy, beware of the

Frederik IV had a close relationship with his younger sister Sophie Hedevig (1677–1735). This portrait was painted by Bénoît le Coffre in 1696. There were lengthy negotiations regarding a possible marriage between Sophie Hedevig and the Habsburger and later emperor Joseph I, but such a marriage ultimately proved to be an impossibility because she refused to convert to Catholicism. Subsequently, in 1698, Christian V tried in vain to get Sophie Hedevig married to the very young King Charles XII of Sweden.

old nobility, and retain the incumbent heads of administrative areas. Frederik IV followed the first two pieces of advice but not the last one. On the contrary, in the beginning of his reign he chose to make a number of personnel changes in the administration so he had trusted individuals heading the chancelleries. In the course of a few years, he achieved a level of personal control of the apparatus of power Christian V had never come near.

However, Frederik IV also inherited his father's foreign policy, and in this area, things nearly went seriously wrong. After Charles XII had become King of Sweden, a show-

The Swedish "warrior king" Charles XII, a cousin of Frederik IV. Painted by Axel Sparre in 1715.

down between Sweden on the one hand and Saxony-Poland and Russia on the other hand appeared imminent, and during the period immediately prior to his death, Christian V had negotiated with a view to bringing about a common military action against Sweden. An agreement was reached according to which Saxony-Poland would attack first, and the agreement was signed by Russia immediately before Christian V's death. Frederik IV had thus inherited an obligation to go to war, but he, too, was provoked by the similarly named Duke of Gottorp, Duke Friedrich (or Frederik) and the very young Swedish king, who were determined to go to war. A relevant aspect of this situation was that Charles XII and Friedrich were both sons of Christian V's sisters and thus cousins of Frederik IV.

When, in February 1700, Frederik IV learned that Polish forces had attacked Riga, which was then Swedish, he sent an army of eighteen thousand men towards Gottorp. The Danish troops conquered and destroyed a number of the Duke's newly built fortifications and besieged the fortified town of Tönning, where, in May, they were joined by an army of Swedish and Netherlandic troops. Frederik IV went down there himself, but there were never any particularly dramatic developments. However, Poland's Augustus II (Augustus the

Portrait of Frederik IV in his coronation cape, flanked by the lions of the coat of arms of the realm. Painted at his anointment, probably by Bénoit le Coffre.

Frederik IV's anoint-
ment on 15 April
1700. Just after the
brief war had begun,
Frederik IV and Queen
Louise were anointed
in Frederiksborg Pal-

Strong) failed to conquer Riga, and Russia was busy with its war against Turkey,
so Frederik IV was suddenly alone in facing Sweden and its powerful allies, England and the Dutch Republic.

With the help of a fleet provided by his allies, Charles XII was therefore able to go
ashore on Zealand with twelve thousand men, who besieged Copenhagen. This was

a shock, but just when the situation looked most hopeless, the war was stopped by England and the Dutch Republic, who easily disarmed the Swedish attack. The War of the Spanish Succession was brewing, and the two major powers wished to see the Nordic conflict terminated. On 18 August 1700 at Traventhal House in Holstein, a peace treaty was signed that obliged Denmark to pay considerable war reparations to Gottorp and Frederik IV not to conclude alliances with enemies of Sweden.

ace Church. Gouache (watercolour drawing) by Bendix Grodtsch-illing from 1706, that is, six years after the event.

While this was a peace treaty one could live with, the short war taught Frederik IV an important lesson. It had made it obvious that Christian V's foreign policy had been misguided and that it could be a fatal mistake not to maintain control of the seas in the vicinity of Denmark. For his part, the Swedish king was frustrated by having to give up the prospect of conquering Copenhagen, but on the other hand, he was now free to make war on Russia, and he soon did so. In contrast, Frederik IV contracted smallpox, the same disease that had killed several of his siblings and half-siblings, and went through a very difficult time, but ultimately the King recovered.

Nine years of peace

While large parts of the rest of Europe were at war, Frederik IV sought to gain the greatest possible advantage by keeping Denmark-Norway neutral. He inherited a large amount of state debt that was almost doubled by the short war, but instead of increasing the already heavy tax burden on his subjects, he tightened up the realm's economic administration. Frederik IV took a particular interest in this area; the finances of the state were fully under his personal control. In January 1700, he created a new administrative model for the Chamber of Finance (the Ministry of Finance of the time) to get rid of his father's independently operating finance director, and three years later, the King in reality became his own minister of finance. Correspondingly, he reduced the role of the Privy Council from that of a government council to that of a body that only prepared cases for processing by the so-called chancelleries. In 1706, Frederik IV also removed the actual decision-making procedure from the council so that all decisions were made by the King himself and his cabinet of trusted court officials. He was wise enough not to abstain from receiving continual advice from the administration, but in reality, he imposed his personal absolute power by taking away the right to make decisions from the administrative apparatus. This necessarily meant that a disproportionately large number of matters needed to be processed and decided at Frederik IV's own desk, and he became known for working there until late at night.

It is not easy to say what drove him. A sense of duty was probably a large part of it, but this would have been a duty he felt he had in relation to God and the crown rather than to his subjects. The notion that the King should serve the

Shortly after his accession to the throne, Frederik IV, inspired by Versailles, had his Mirror Cabinet built at Rosenborg, in which visitors can see themselves reflected on the floor, ceiling, and walls. During the Baroque period, mirror cabinets were built as special private royal chambers at a number of royal courts. Frederik IV's bedroom was on the ground floor and was connected to the mirror cabinet by the tower's spiral staircase. In a wall cabinet, he had a collection of erotica, of which only a few miniature paintings are preserved at Rosenborg. It is assumed that his less libertine successor may have had the rest destroyed.

When Frederik
IV visited Venice
in 1709, the city
presented him with
a splendid collection
of glass. To house
this collection,
he created his
so-called glass
cabinet, which was
inspired by the
porcelain room at
Charlottenburg in
Berlin, which he
had visited on his
way home. While
porcelain cabinets
were popular during
the time of Frederik
IV, this is the only
known glass cabinet
in Europe.

people did not gain currency until later. The decisive factor was probably that the King had difficulty trusting those around him. The court was characterised by endless intrigues and by the efforts of various individuals to manoeuvre and position themselves; everyone spoke with exaggerated politeness, but no one trusted others, and Frederik IV's style of government was probably a reflection of the fact that he was a suspicious type who was destined to be at the centre of a paranoid environment.

While Queen Louise was having children, Frederik IV began a relationship with a diplomat's daughter from Brandenburg, Elisabeth Helene von Vieregg, who was a lady-in-waiting of his sister Sophie Hedevig. He installed her in the same house behind Børsen (the Stock Exchange) that Christian V's mistress had lived in, and in 1703, he made her a countess. Helene von Vieregg appears to have been an amusing individual, and all the evidence suggests that she influenced the King to a much greater extent than the Queen did. According to a letter written by her father, the King discreetly married her, and this was a real innovation, for while kings had had mistresses since time immemorial, polygamy had not previously been seen. For ordinary people, it was in fact a crime that was punishable by death, but the absolute monarch was above the law and had no earthly instances above him.

In 1704, Frederik IV set forth to undertake the obligatory tour of Norway. At that point, the King had ruled that country for nearly five years, and the visit must have generated a certain excitement. A traditional route for royal visits had already been established: first around the southern coast, then up to Trondheim and down through Guldbrandsdalen (the Guldbrand Valley) to Christiania (Oslo). In Bergen, however, the King received the sad news that Helene von Vieregg had died after having given birth to their first child—a son who died eight months later. Frederik IV arranged a magnificent funeral for the countess in connection with which he had the bells in three of Copenhagen's churches rung for three hours. He believed that the deaths of his mistress and her child were God's punishment, and he stayed away from operas and masquerade balls for some time thereafter. There are signs that he even attempted to be a good husband to Queen Louise; for example, he and the Queen had a common bedroom—something that was not at all typical for royal couples of the age—furnished for the two of them in Rosenborg.

As long as it proved to be possible to maintain neutrality in the area of foreign policy, Frederik IV's most important priorities were reducing the state debt and strengthening both the army and the navy. An innovation was the creation of a militia of fifteen thousand peasants who could supplement the standing—and extremely expensive—army of professional soldiers, who were rented out to warring countries to the greatest possible extent during the years of neutrality. Gottorp remained a constant problem, though one of the King's two hostile cousins, Duke Friedrich, was killed when he was making war on Poland together with the other cousin, Charles XII. Tensions increased in 1706, when the Prince-Bishop of Lübeck died, and both Christian August, who was at the head of the new regency government in Gottorp, and Frederik IV's brother, Prince Carl, could argue that they had a right to inherit the Prince-Bishop's title. Christian August marched into Eutin to let himself be hailed as the successor, and Frederik IV threatened to go to war over the matter, but in the end, he chose not to, as he was too poorly prepared. This was a period in which Charles XII was celebrating one triumph after another as a military commander, and defending his brother's interests would have involved Frederik IV in a new war with Sweden.

Despite the threat of war, Frederik IV allowed himself nine months to revisit his beloved Italy in 1708 and 1709. This was made possible by the fact that the army of Charles XII had finished beating Augustus the Strong—first in Poland, where he was deposed as King, and then in Saxony—and had begun a new campaign against Russia. For this reason, Denmark-Norway was not immediately threatened, and Frederik IV now took a pleasure trip despite the fact that such a thing was fairly unheard-of for a ruling absolute monarch. Not surprisingly, the King put the business of government on standby; he did not authorize his ministers to make decisions in his absence. This time, too, he travelled incognito, but this was just a formality that enabled the King to avoid the etiquette that would otherwise had been associated with a royal visit—given that the King was travelling with a retinue of eighty persons, it was fairly obvious that he was more than a "Count of Oldenburg." The King's main goal was Venice, and from there the tour took the King via Ferrara and Bologna to Florence, where, as has been mentioned, Frederik IV again saw Maddalena Trenta, who had entered a nunnery and was now called Maria.

During his visit to Italy, Frederik IV corresponded with the very young Charlotte Helene von Schindel, who had been a kind of lady-in-waiting to Helene von

A very fine painted fan in ivory that Frederik IV bought on his second journey to Italy and presented to Queen Louise. On this side, one can see a group of musicians in a park, on the other a scene featuring shepherds and shepherdesses. During the eighteenth century, the use of handheld fans was at its height, and there was an advanced language associated with fans that allowed a woman to send a myriad of wordless signals.

Vieregg. After the King had returned to Denmark in 1709, she acquired more or less official status as the King's mistress—as her former superior had—and was given a few Zealand estates, but Frederik IV refrained from marrying her, though there is supposed to have been a brief period during which he entertained thoughts of doing so. In any event, he lost interest in her at the latest in 1711, when he met Anna Sophie Reventlow.

The Great Northern War

Shortly after he had returned to Denmark, Frederik IV chose to declare war on Sweden. There was a good reason for this: After a series of great triumphs as a military commander, Charles XII had finally suffered a significant defeat by Russia. Frederik IV's hope was that he would now be able to win back the areas that had been lost on the other side of the Øresund, and the plan was that Russia and Augustus the Strong—whom Frederik IV had visited in Saxony on his way home from Italy and with whom he had concluded a new alliance at that time—would attack the Swedes simultaneously this time.

As during the Scanian War, Denmark-Norway's plan now was to reconquer Scania, Blekinge, and Halland and simultaneously attack from the Norwegian border, and on 12 November 1709, a Danish main force of fifteen thousand men went ashore near the fishing hamlet of Rå in Scania—the place where Christian V had gone ashore in 1676. However, Frederik IV had just as little success with his plans for reconquest of the area as his father had had, for on 10 March 1710, the Danes suffered a crushing defeat at the Battle of Helsingborg that in reality decided the future of Scania, Blekinge, and Halland. More than half of the men who fought on the Danish side were lost (five thousand killed or wounded, just under three thousand taken prisoner), and the rest of the army subsequently had to be evacuated. As a result of poor organisation, the attack from Norway had never gotten started, and this had enabled the Swedes to dedicate more troops to securing a victory in Scania.

The war continued in Northern Germany, where Danish forces suffered a bloody defeat by the Swedish general Stenbock at Gadebusch in December 1712. Coordination with the Saxon forces did not work, and the Russian forces did not interfere despite the fact that they were nearby when the battle took place. Af-

Stade Erobret d. 6 Septem

Frederik IV accepts Stade's surrender in 1712. Stade is a Northern German town in what was then the state of Bremen-Verden, which had been conquered by Sweden during the Torstenson War in the time of Christian IV. The Swedes had to surrender the town to Frederik IV after a siege lasting some weeks and a major bombardment. The painting is attributed to G. P. Rugendas.

ter this lesson, Frederik IV took charge as a military commander to a greater extent than he had previously. He pulled his troops back and organised the defence of Jutland while Stenbock prepared to invade from the south as Sweden had done twice during the preceding century. This time, it proved to be a bad idea, as Frederik IV, by bringing strong diplomatic pressure to bear, was able to get his allies to go after Stenbock, who ended up, with his army, having to seek sanctuary in the fortified town of Tönning in Gottorp. Previously, on the order of Charles XII, but without any meaningful reason, the Swedes had burned the town of Altona (the southernmost town under the Danish crown) to the ground. A few months later, Stenbock was forced to surrender, and this was the beginning of the end of Sweden's many years of presence in Northern Germany. For Frederik IV, this meant that he succeeded where his father had not: in securing possession of all of Schleswig. By opening Tönning to the Swedes, the Gottorpers had violated the neutrality they had claimed to be maintaining in the war, in which they had attempted to keep all their options open after the Swedish defeat in Russia. Their violation of neutrality made it possible for Frederik IV to

Self-portrait of the captured Swedish army commander Magnus Stenbock that shows him holding a plea for release. After he surrendered in the fortified town of Tönning in 1713, Stenbock was imprisoned in the Citadel in Copenhagen, where he expressed himself using his artistic talents. The picture shows him in what looks like a hen-yard, with the fortifications in the background. It is possible that he inserted himself and the fortifications into an existing landscape painting to express his humility in a humorous fashion. His plea to be released was in vain, for Stenbock died in prison in 1717.

Gilded lead bust of Peter the Great, the Emperor of Russia (1672–1725) Peter the Great was Frederik IV's ally in the Great Northern War but otherwise as different from the Danish king as he could have been. The czar was very literally a great man and was known for his rather coarse manners, while Frederik IV was a small man who paid great attention to etiquette. The bust was made by B. C. D. Rastrelli.

get the major powers to agree to let him keep the parts of Gottorp that were in Schleswig.

Frederik IV wished to undertake a new attack in Scania, but he was prevented from doing so by the great sea powers, who preferred the existing power relationships in the Øresund region. For the time being, Denmark could help to chase the Swedes out of Northern Germany completely as part of an alliance

Tordenskjold managed to sabotage Charles XII's first campaign in Norway when, at the Battle of Dynekilen on 8 July 1716, he attacked a Swedish transport fleet and its escort. A large number of Swedish ships were captured and destroyed, and an unknown number of soldiers killed. What was most important was that the ships' cargo of heavy artillery was prevented from reaching Charles XII's army in the field, and only a few days later, as a result of this attack, the Swedes were no longer in Norway.

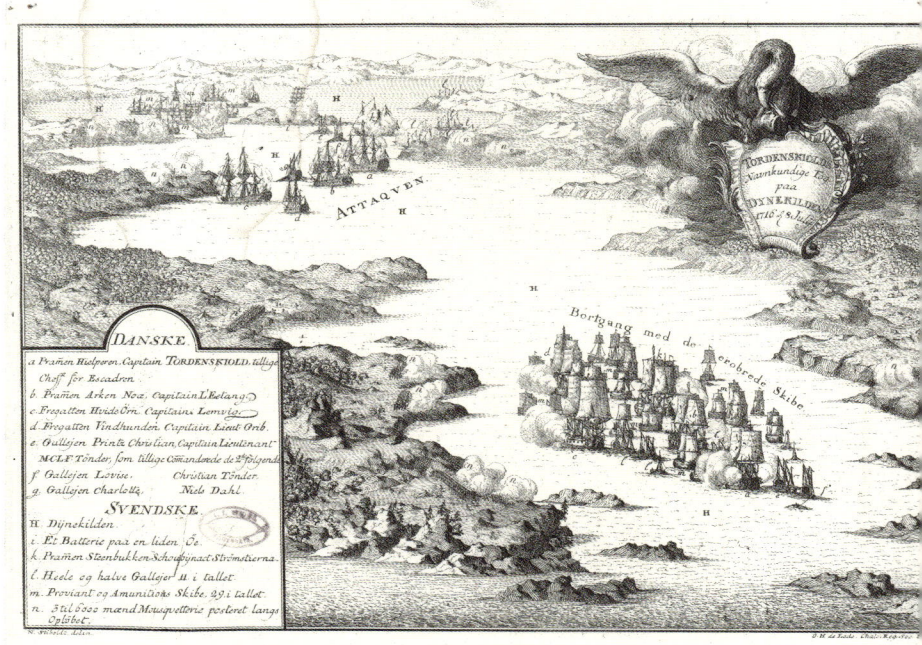

with Prussia and Hanover, and this project was successfully completed in the course of 1715 and 1716. The Danish navy played an important role by defeating the Swedish navy in connection with the siege of Stralsund, and after the Swedish defeat, Frederik IV promised a generous bounty to any captain who could capture Charles XII on his way to Sweden. No one succeeded in this despite the fact that determined efforts were made—notably by the young Norwegian frigate captain Peter Wessel, who had made a positive impression during the war and in 1716 was made a nobleman under the name Tordenskjold.

In 1716, there appeared to be a new opportunity to attack Scania, Blekinge, and Halland, this time with support from the Russian emperor, who arrived in Copenhagen in the summer of 1716 with an army comprising no fewer than thirty thousand individuals. There are a number of good stories about Peter the Great's time in Copenhagen. According to one of these stories, the Russian

Cup of glass commemorating the death of Charles XII on 11 December 1718. The cup's decorations include a depiction of the terrain around Fredriksten. The fatal shot probably came from the fortress, but it could have come from the Swedes' own ranks—and it might even have been fired on the orders of Frederik (I) of Hesse, who became Charles XII's successor on the Swedish throne.

giant, standing on top of the Round Tower, bragged to the slightly built Danish king that he would be able to get any one of his subjects to jump from the tower simply by giving an order to this effect. To this, Frederik IV is supposed to have responded that he, Frederik IV, would be able to sleep in the home of any farmer in his kingdoms without having to fear anything.

Next spread: View of Fredensborg Slot, as it appeared in 1739. Gouache by J. J. Bruun.

Statuette of
Frederik IV, made
to commemorate
the peace treaty
concluded at
Frederiksborg
in 1720. The
goddess of victory
is hovering over
him and holding
a victory wreath
while she blows a
trumpet from which
a banner flutters
bearing the words
"May the King's
joy, the country's
peace, and the well-
being of the people
endure." Under the
King's feet lies a
male figure who
represents evil.
Silver with gilded
areas, executed by
Peter Klein.

The common attack never became a reality, and the reason for this was probably that the Russian czar was carrying on independent negotiations with the Swedish government, which was of course doing all it could to split the Danish-Russian alliance. Sweden even got Peter the Great to agree to support a Swedish attack on Norway in return for being allowed to take over the Swedish areas on the Eastern Baltic coast, but this agreement turned out not to be relevant. This was because Charles XII believed he was strong enough to conquer Norway, which would be the battleground contested in the war's final phase, on his own. The Swedish king took Christiania in the course of his first campaign in 1716 but pulled back when reinforcements arrived from Denmark.

During the following years, the contested sites were Frederikshald (now Halden) and the fortress of Fredriksten, and during this phase of the war, the Swedish operations were interfered with several times by Tordenskjold. It was also Tordenskjold who came to Copenhagen and gave Frederik IV the welcome news that his cousin Charles XII had been struck in the temple by a bullet while he was inspecting his forces' dispositions in December 1718. The warrior king was thirty-six years old when he died, and he had been at war almost constantly since he had become King of Sweden as a youth. If his diplomatic wisdom had been as great as his talents as a military commander, the result would probably have been different, but with his death, the Great Northern War and Sweden's time as a major power had in reality both ended.

It took time to establish the conditions of the peace, which for Frederik IV ended up being as good as was politically possible. He acquired no new territory other than Gottorp's areas in Schleswig, but he received substantial compensation for giving up the other areas he had conquered in what is today Northern Germany. Also, Sweden had to give up the right to exemption from paying the Øresund customs duties, which provided Denmark with a welcome extra source of income, and promise never again to support Gottorp against Denmark. The peace treaty was signed at Frederiksborg Palace on 3 July 1720, and when Sweden and Russia signed a peace treaty the following year, the Great Northern War was formally over. In a wider perspective, the peace meant that the old Danish-Swedish fight for mastery of the Baltic Sea region was over, as the strengthened positions of Russia and Poland created a new balance of power. For Frederik IV's subjects, this was a colossal relief; while the war had been fought outside Denmark, Danes at home had had to pay a high price in the form

Gold cup bearing Frederik IV's initials in diamonds. The cup was a present for Count U. A. Holstein, who was married to Anna Sophie's half-sister, Christine Sophie Reventlow. The King gave the count this cup to thank him and his wife for their help in connection with the abduction of Anna Sophie from Clausholm. After the Great Northern War, Holstein was even made a grand chancellor, but his time in this office came to an end when Christian VI acceded to the throne and removed him and other relatives of Anna Sophie from their official positions.

of war taxes. Now, though, it had proved possible to secure a peace agreement that would endure for the rest of the century, and to celebrate this, Frederik IV built a palace he named Fredensborg ("the Peace Palace").

On both of his journeys to Italy Frederik IV experienced the carnival in Venice, which inspired him to arrange masquerade balls at home in Denmark. He had his costumes sewn from materials from Italy, and they often represented caricatured, fantastic versions of well-known features. This costume let the King appear as a servant, but it is sewn from the most expensive materials imaginable—mostly cloth of silver and cloth of gold. The gold fringes on the knee breeches must have granted the King's dance steps a particular flair.

Queen Louise
portrayed by J. S.
du Wahl not long
before her death.

The abduction

Of course, the war years put the King under an enormous amount of pressure, but despite the constant struggle to ensure the adequacy of state finances and the military organisation, Frederik IV also found time to live out the romantic adventure of his life.

Frederik IV as portrayed by J. S. du Wahl around 1720. The war scene in the background is intended to help posterity to associate the King with the war and its successful conclusion.

As is so often the case, war had been accompanied by disease, and in 1711, plague broke out in Copenhagen and killed a third of the city's approximately seventy thousand inhabitants. While the bodies were piling up in the streets, the court wisely moved to Jutland, and at a masquerade ball for the Jutlandic nobility at Koldinghus, Frederik IV met the eighteen-year-old noblewoman Anna Sophie Reventlow. The King was deeply smitten, and the young countess by no means rejected his overtures, but her mother had no intention of letting her daughter join the ranks of the King's mistresses. The following summer, however, Frederik IV felt that it was time to transform fantasy into reality, so he travelled to the estate of Clausholm in Djursland, where Anna Sophie had grown up and now lived. Her mother was appropriately hospitable but did not let the King get near her daughter, so he travelled on to Skanderborg without having gotten what he had come for. In Skanderborg, however, he met Anna Sophie Reventlow's half-sister, who assured him that his love for Anna Sophie was requited, and two days later, the King again presented himself at Clausholm. This time, he did not leave empty-handed, for with help from the local servants, who received generous bribes, he succeeded in smuggling his beloved into his carriage after the visit. The King then returned to Skanderborg as quickly as possible, and when Anna Sophie Reventlow stepped out of the carriage, Frederik IV appointed her Duchess of Schleswig. With this, she was no longer only a noblewoman but of princely rank, and that same day, she agreed to a morganatic marriage to the King. Formally, the ceremony performed that day did not constitute a valid marriage, for it was performed by a young theologian who was not yet an ordained priest, so it appears possible that Frederik IV just wanted her to believe that they were married. For her part, Anna Sophie may have insisted on marriage as a precondition for entering into a relationship with the King.

The newly married couple spent a few happy weeks on the estate of Boller near Horsens before Frederik IV had to travel to his military headquarters in Holstein. His letters bear witness to the fact that he was deeply in love, and on top of this, he could celebrate military success when his troops conquered Bremen shortly thereafter. In September, the King returned to plague-ravaged Copenhagen after having been away for fifteen months and was joined there the following month by Anna Sophie, whom he later installed in an appropriately grand residence on Slotsholmen. He also gave her the estate Vallø south of Køge as well as several estates in Holstein.

When Frederik IV and Peter the Great were waiting for Stenbock to surrender in 1713, both Anna Sophie and Empress Catherine were transported to the duchies to keep their husbands company. The two women were both pregnant and must have had much to talk about (in German, which they both spoke), for the Czarina had first been in a morganatic marriage with Peter the Great and, like

Anna Sophie, was not from a princely family. In fact, there were a number of examples of morganatic marriages in European princely houses during this period, but this by no means meant that the widespread condemnation of such marriages came to an end.

On the occasion of Frederik IV's fiftieth birthday celebration in 1721, his sister Sophie Hedevig presented him with two small paintings of wreaths of flowers that she had painted herself. One has Frederik IV's monogram in the centre, the other an oval mirror. It was painted at Vemmetofte, where she and Prince Carl took up residence in protest against the King's decision to make Anna Sophie Queen, and the present appears to be a subtle way of asking whether Frederik IV could look in the mirror and then claim that he had acted in accordance with what should be expected of a king.

The years with Queen Anna Sophie

On 15 March 1721, Queen Louise died, and one could hardly say her husband was crushed by grief. The funeral took place on 3 April, and the following day, Frederik IV entered into a regular marriage with Anna Sophie. The initial effect of this was to indicate that Anna Sophie was now the King's properly wedded wife, which gave her a status similar to that of Christian IV's wife Kirsten Munk. Only a few months later, however, Frederik IV invited the royal family and the highest officials to a hastily arranged meeting at Frederiksberg Palace, where, to the surprise of all, he crowned Anna Sophie and declared her Queen of Denmark-Norway. Making a queen out of a woman who was not from a royal family was a radical break with precedent, and the King's immediate family refused to accept this enhancement of Anna Sophie's status. The King's siblings, Prince Carl and Princess Sophie Hedevig, left the court in protest and established their residence at Vemmetofte Manor on Stevns, and Crown Prince Christian (VI) reacted even more negatively. He had seen his mother be set aside and spend many unhappy years in Denmark, and because of this, he never recognised Anna Sophie's status as Queen despite the fact that Frederik IV did much to bring about a reconciliation between himself and the Crown Prince—probably not least because he was concerned about how his wife might be treated after his death.

It is difficult to say to what extent Anna Sophie herself had political influence, but the Queen's relatives benefited from her new status. A series of appointments and promotions of family members and their supporters caused many to mutter about "the Reventlow gang" that became very influential at the court during the years that followed. However, Frederik IV's changes to the state administration were not undertaken solely to show favouritism to his Queen's family, for after the war he implemented a change of course with regard to foreign policy. He now sought to establish ties with England and France rather than Russia, and this of course meant giving the cold shoulder to the officials who had represented the Russia-oriented alliance policies. In 1724, rumours began circulating with regard to corruption among Anna Sophie's relatives, who were allegedly taking bribes in return for presenting requests for appointments to official posts or other expressions of favour to the Queen, and Frederik IV found it necessary to appoint a committee to investigate these allegations. The result of the investigation was a number of firings and lawsuits against prominent officials, but we cannot know whether the investigation incriminated the Queen, as Christian VI had the committee's files destroyed—in itself, this suggests, if anything, that the Queen was not incriminated.

Fredensborg Slot was inaugurated in 1722, and the royal couple subsequently loved to spend time there. The painting shows an amusing scene in which Frederik IV and Queen Anna Sophie are fishing at Anglehuset (the Fishing House) down at the lake Esrum Sø; the palace is seen in the background. The man in the water appears to have fallen out of his rowboat, and the servants are pulling him ashore using the Queen's fishing line. It might well be that a funny incident had inspired the painting of this scene. The saluting "warship" on the lake must be a rowboat fitted with props. Painted by A. E. du Wllarst in about 1727.

In 1725, Frederik IV introduced open audience times during which all his subjects, of high rank and low, could approach His Majesty. Between ten and eleven o'clock in the morning, one could come to the palace, present one's case to the King, and hand over a written account of the situation, regarding which the King could subsequently make a decision. People were directly encouraged to complain if they felt they had been victimised by illegal actions, and the measure was no doubt motivated by Frederik IV's deep mistrust of his officials. Of course, it made the King even more popular among the populace than he had been previously.

Frederik IV's love for Queen Anna Sophie was apparently undying, but life at court became less festive during her time as Queen. This had to do in part with

Gold writing set with Frederik IV's initials, made by Frederik Babritius in the 1720s.

the heartbreaking series of small coffins the King and Queen had to bury. Anna Sophie gave birth to a total of six children, the first two of whom died in infancy while the third was stillborn. Of the three children to whom she subsequently gave birth as Queen, none lived to an age of more than one year. The King and Queen must have believed their marriage to be cursed, so it is understandable that during Frederik IV's last years the royal couple turned to religion.

The Pietist interpretation of Christianity had won more and more ground during the reign of Frederik IV, and the King was not unaffected. Pietism demanded an emotional worshipping of God that was to be expressed in the form of piety and

Anna Sophie is being brought to heaven by Christ, accompanied by a lady-in-waiting bearing his cross. Up there Frederik IV is waiting, sitting next to an empty chair with Anna Sophie's initials on it. Unknown artist.

When Fredensborg was to be built, Christian IV's house "Sparepenge" across from Frederiksborg Palace was torn down so that the materials could be reused for the new palace. On the cleared ground, Frederik IV established magnificent baroque gardens that were recreated in the 1990s. He established other pleasure gardens at locations including Odense Palace, Koldinghus, and Sønderborg Palace and of course at Frederiksberg. It is not for nothing that Frederik IV has been called the greatest creator of gardens in Denmark's history.

brotherly love, and in practice, it resulted in an increased interest in schooling and in providing for the poor. Several of Frederik IV's projects were conceived in the spirit of Pietism. These include the poverty ordinance of 1708 as well as Hans Egede's departure for Greenland in 1721, which marked the beginning of the Christianisation of Greenland—and was of course also a profit-motivated colonisation project. There was also the establishment of 240 so-called ryt-terskoler ("cavalry schools") in the country's twelve cavalry districts during the years 1721–27 with the purpose of improving the common people's bibli-cal knowledge. One could also mention the founding of Vajsenhuset (the Royal Orphan House) for children without parents in 1727, but the most extreme ex-pression of the King's religious conversion in his later years was the Sabbath ordinance he decreed about six months before he died. This ordinance imposed harsh penalties for failing to attend worship services and forbade all forms of worldly activities on holidays. It anticipated the serious religiosity that would characterise the reign of Christian VI.

The great Copenhagen fire of September 1728 was believed by many—doubt-less including the royal couple—to be God's punishment. The cathedral, the Trinitatis Church, and many other prominent buildings went up in flames; in all, two-fifths of the capital city burned, and of course, the mood at court was nec-essarily affected by this. It is quite telling that Frederik IV did not find it appro-priate to provide support for the construction of a new theatre as a replacement for the theatre in Ny Adelgade (then Grønnegade), which had burnt down and in previous years had offered a home to Ludvig Holberg's amusing comedies.

It was a particular problem for the King that he could not protect Anna Sophie against the Crown Prince's hatred, though he had gotten the Crown Prince to sign a testament regarding her position as a widow. This problem may have also played a role in the thoughts Frederik IV in fact entertained with regard to abdicat-ing and retiring to Fredensborg Palace to make his peace with God. Such an abdi-cation never became a reality, however, for the King was still working too much, and he became seriously ill during an inspection tour his physician had urgently advised him not to undertake. After having lain in his sickbed in Schleswig for a few weeks, he attempted the journey to Copenhagen but only reached Odense, where Frederik IV died in the small hours of the morning on 12 October 1730—the day after he had turned fifty-nine years old. The Queen was with him until the end, and they both knew hard times were coming for her after his death.

Indeed, she was not permitted to participate in the funeral, but Christian VI punished her less harshly than he might have wished to. After all, she was from a fine and extremely wealthy family, so Queen Anna Sophie was spared prison, but she had to spend the rest of her days under house arrest at Clausholm—the childhood home from which Frederik IV had abducted her many years previously.

The legacy

In his memorial speech at the University of Copenhagen, Ludvig Holberg described Frederik IV as a man who "believed it was proper for a king to die standing, believed that as torches can be kept burning by constantly being shaken

Table with
Florentine mosaic.
All decorations
are polished
semiprecious stones
inlaid in a plate
of black marble.
The table was
made in Florence
and presented to
Frederik IV when he
visited the Grand
Duke of Tuscany
during his second
journey through
Italy.

one's strength is maintained by constantly being used but diminished by the interruption of work." This is undoubtedly true, but the colossal pressure he was under to work was the price he had to pay for his personal exercise of power.

Some have criticised Frederik IV for his headstrong style of governing. He could lose himself in details at the expense of the whole, for example by checking budgets for accounting errors, and it is also well-known that in several cases, the military command structure suffered because the King insisted on making decisions himself. Frederik IV was certainly not trusting, and it is hardly without any justification that he has been described as paranoid—for example because of the political testament in which the King, impressed by the fall of the Swedish absolute monarchy, warned his son against the old nobility.

In general, however, posterity has had a hard time seeing the reign of Frederik IV as anything but a success. The state was well administered in all areas, and it cannot be denied that the King succeeded in protecting the security of the realm. The King's kingdoms and lands were not ravaged by the dramatic battles that transpired during his reign, and the King succeeded in eliminating the problem of Gottorp and securing lasting peace. For this reason, it is actually remarkable that Frederik IV has not left more of an impression as a historical figure. One explanation for this could be a lack of clarity, for one can associate very different things with him. The King's dutiful and hardworking life does not immediately appear to harmonise with the King's southern abandon and his controversial love life, and his hard-won military successes are nearly invisible in the context of a historical retrospective. It is difficult to relate to the fact that Gottorp in Schleswig was once such a great prize, and while Frederik IV's palaces are pretty, they are, after all, more anonymous than Christian IV's buildings. Not even a king's story is told if the plot is too unclear.

The King would hardly have thought much about such matters himself, for in his bleak last years, his thoughts are likely to have been focused on the fate of Queen Anna Sophie and his own soul. However, Frederik IV would probably have found it strange if he had known that there would come a day when almost no Danes remembered his name but all Danes knew Tordenskjold's.

SUGGESTIONS FOR FURTHER READING

Marie Hvidt, Frederik IV – *En letsindig alvorsmand,* Gads Forlag 2004.
A well-written and entertaining biography that is both thoroughly researched and fictionalised.

Henning Dehn-Nielsen, *Frederik 4. – Tordenskiolds konge,* Forlaget Sesam 2001.
A briefer, concise historical biography divided by theme.

Dan H. Andersen, *Peter Wessel Tordenskiold,* Lindhardt og Ringhof 2015.
A comprehensive and exciting portrayal of the naval hero's dramatic life.

Michael Bregnsbo, *Til venstre hånd – Danske kongers elskerinder,* Gyldendal 2010.
A very sober and scholarly treatment of a juicy subject. The book's particular focus is on the mistress as a political actor in Danish history.

Ulla Kjær, Bente Scavenius, and Christine Waage Rasmussen, *Fredensborg – Slot og slotshave,* Gads Forlag 2013.
A richly illustrated work in a large format that illuminates Frederik IV's most important building projects from all sides.

kongernessamling.dk

Frederik IV
King on his own terms

Copyright © 2017
The Royal Danish Collection and Historika / Gads Forlag A/S

ISBN: 978-87-93229-75-4
First edition, first print run

Printed in Lithuania

Text: Jens Gunni Busck
Edited by Birgit Jenvold
Translated from Danish by Peter Sean Woltemade
Cover and graphic design Lene Nørgaard, Le Bureau
Printed by Clemenstrykkeriet, Lithuania

Illustrations:
Front page, p. 2, 4 (photo: Kit Weiss), 7, 8-9 (photo: Iben Kaufmann), 10, 12, 13, 15, 16, 18-19, 20, 22, 24-25, 26 (photo: Jens Lindhe), 29 (photo: Jens Lindhe), 30, 33, 34-35, 36, 37, 39, 40-41, 42 (photo: Kit Weiss), 44, 45, 46, 47, 49, 50, 51, 52, 53, 56-57: The Royal Danish Collection, p. 23: National-museum Stockholm, p. 38: Igor Dymov/Dreamstime.com, p. 55: The Royal Library.